Whiskey Prayers: The Journal
Healing • Reflection • Recovery

JAI Lewis

Whiskey Prayers and Midnight Moments

This is a work of nonfiction. Names, details, and identifying characteristics
have been changed where necessary to protect privacy.

First Edition 2026

Published by JAI Lewis Writes
Atlanta, Georgia

Cover design by JAI Lewis
Interior formatting by JAI Lewis

ISBN: 979-8-9953317-2-8

Printed in the United States of America

Dedication

For My Mother –

Whose strength still colors my world. I see your favorite shade of purple in the fabric of my life. The dream is no longer a whisper — it is becoming.
Thank you for planting a pen in my spirit and teaching me that words could carry weight when my voice felt small.

For My Father –

 Your steadiness shaped me. You taught me discipline, discretion, and the quiet power of endurance.
Thank you for giving me a life strong enough to build from.

For My Son –

My reason and my reminder. You are why I keep choosing forward.
You are the why beneath my becoming. I pray the life I fight for becomes the foundation you stand on. I hope this book leaves you braver, stronger, and unafraid of your own becoming.

For My Brother –

Thank you for being a steady part of my foundation.
I hope this story builds something that honors where we started – and where we are both still going.

For My Family –

Thank you for the foundation, the history, and the name I carry forward.

Preface

This journal was created as a companion to Whiskey Prayers and Midnight Moments.

Writing became one of the tools that helped me process my experiences, understand my emotions, and move toward healing. What began as private reflection slowly became structure—space to sit with difficult questions, to notice patterns, and to give language to moments that once felt impossible to explain.

Over time, those quiet pages became a form of soul work. Not polished work. Not perfect work. Just the steady practice of showing up, paying attention, and learning the rhythm of my own mind.

This journal is an invitation to do the same.

These pages offer an invitation to pause and look inward. They create space for reflection, healing, and deeper understanding. Some prompts may feel familiar. Others may ask you to sit with thoughts you have avoided or emotions you have carried quietly for years. Take your time with them. There is no correct pace and no perfect response.

What matters is that the page becomes a place where your thoughts can land without interruption.

Writing helped me notice the architecture of my own patterns—the way certain fears repeated themselves, the way certain moments of clarity appeared when I slowed down enough to see them. Over time, those observations became tools: ways to recognize triggers, restore balance, and return to myself when life felt unsteady.

That is the spirit behind this journal.

You don't need perfect words here. You don't need polished language or carefully edited sentences.

You only need the willingness to sit with the page and discover your own truth.

Author's Note

This journal was created as a companion to Whiskey Prayers and Midnight Moments,
but it also stands on its own.
The memoir tells the story.
This space is where your story begins.

Healing rarely happens in perfect sentences or tidy explanations. Sometimes it begins
in fragments — a thought written down at midnight, a truth you finally allow yourself
to say out loud, a quiet moment where you choose honesty instead of silence.

For years I searched for language strong enough to hold the weight of what I was
surviving. Therapy helped me understand. Recovery helped me stabilize. But the
deeper work — the soul work — began when I started listening to myself.
That is what this journal is for.
It is not here to diagnose you.
It is not here to judge you.
It is here to give you space.
Space to reflect.
Space to question.
Space to tell the truth about what you carry and what you hope to release.

Mental health conversations often stop at labels or clinical definitions. Those tools
matter, but healing is bigger than terminology. It lives in self-awareness, reflection,
cultural context, faith, discipline, and the quiet courage to keep becoming.

Use these pages however you need them.
Write the truth.
Write without apology.
Write what silence has been holding.
Write through the midnight — and into the morning.
Your story deserves room to breathe.

— JAI Lewis

HOW TO USE THIS JOURNAL

Each page contains a short reflection and a writing prompt.
Use the space on each page to reflect and give your thoughts a place to land.
Move through the prompts at your own pace.
Write freely.
Write truly.
Write with intention

This is where the truth starts breathing.

Here, we talk about the real stuff — the things most people are too afraid to say out loud: the good, the bad, and all the messy-in-between.

1. Glam Up, Glam Down

Some days I beat my face with the makeup brush. Other days I couldn't find myself

Prompt:

What role has makeup or outward presentation played in your survival? Write about a time you showed up styled but shattered. What did you need underneath it all?

2. The Mirror Lies

I starred at a stranger until I became her. Some reflections are nothing but echoes of survival.

Prompt:
What lies have mirrors, people, or trauma convinced you to believe? Write your truth back into that reflection.

3. Velvet Rage, Diamond Heart

I raged with softness and healed with heart.

Prompt:
What emotions were you taught to bury that you are finally ready to name?
Let your anger, tenderness, or grief speak in this space.

4. Addiction Wore Lipstick Too

They saw pretty. I was drowning. I needed an anchor.

Prompt:
What coping mechanisms looked polished from the outside but were silently hurting you inside? What mask are you ready to take off?

5. Bruised, Not Broken

Yes, I cracked. Yes, I bled. But I did not break.

Prompt:
Write about a moment you didn't think you would survive, but did. What did that survival cost you? And what did it teach you?

6. The Soft Violence of Healing

Healing didn't scream. It whispered and shattered everything I thought I was.

Prompt:
Describe a time when healing felt like loss instead of progress. What did you have to let go of that hurt more than the trauma itself?

7. Healing Ain't Pretty

My healing was ugly, loud, and honest, but was mine.

Prompt:
What's the real, unfiltered truth about your healing journey? Write it like no one's watching — no edits, no filter, just you.

8. I Left Pieces of Myself Everywhere

I scattered versions of me trying to be whole.

Prompt:
Where did you leave pieces of yourself in people, places, roles, or survival modes? Write them down, then write one piece you are ready to take back.

____
____
____
____
____
____
____
____
____
____
____
____
____
____
____
____
____
____
____
____
____
____
____
____

9. Dancing on the Edge of Becoming

Becoming didn't feel like a glam-up. It felt like a breakdown in motion.

Prompt:

What parts of you are still shifting? Write about the fear and the beauty in your becoming.

10. Healing Felt Like Satin

I didn't just survive. I started to look good doing it.

Prompt:
What does your healing look like when it feels good? Write about your
glow-up moments — not just physically, but emotionally. What makes
you feel divine, feminine, and finally free?

11. Containment Is Care

No filter, no fear.
Release is not avoidance —it's survival.
I am not writing for pretty. I'm writing for freedom.

Prompt:
Keeping everything inside isn't strength — it's pressure. Journaling creates a container where truth can exist without judgment, interruption, or consequence. What's one truth you never written or said out loud? Use this space. Be unfiltered. Be fearless.

12. The Diary of a Beautiful Disaster

Even in the wreckage, there are wild flowers.

Prompt:
What parts of your chaos still carry beauty? Write a love letter to the most misunderstood version of you.

13. Heels On, Hurts Off

I've cried in stilettos and smiled in sweatpants. Either way, I'm still here.

Prompt:

Write about your duality — the fierce, the soft, the undone, and the unstoppable. Where do you show up for yourself, no matter what you're wearing?

14. From Surviving to Thriving

I don't just breathe now. I live!

Prompt:
What does thriving look like for you — not for everyone else? Write
about your joy, your freedom, your future.

15. Glam vs. Truth

They complimented my glow. They didn't see my grief.

Prompt:
What does "put together" look like when you're falling apart? What's
one part of yourself that looked polished but was secretly torn in
pieces.

16. Mascara-Streaked Survival

I didn't cry pretty. I cried through lashes, liner, and lipstick.

Prompt:
What part of your pain broke through your nail polish? Write about a time when the tears didn't care how "together" you looked.

17. Puffy Eyes and a Hangover

My face was swollen, but my spirit was screaming. And somehow, I still got up.

Prompt:
Describe a time when you woke up drained, raw, and tired of pretending. What were you carrying — and what did you leave behind when you finally rose?

18. She Believed, Eventually

Confidence didn't come all at once. I built it between breakdowns.

Prompt:
Write about the version of you who wasn't sure - but still showed up.
What helped you begin believing in yourself little by little?

19. Strength You Can't See

The strongest thing I ever did was keep going.

Prompt:
What's one moment of quiet strength you've never acknowledged?
Write about the times you didn't give up, even when no one noticed —
not even you.

20. Masterpiece in Progress

Unfinished, unfiltered, and still art.

Prompt:

Where in your life are you still under construction? What parts of you feel incomplete — and what would wholeness look like? Write about what it means to be unfinished and still worthy.

21. Give Your Thoughts Space

Even strong minds get tired. Some thoughts don't need answers. They need a soft place to land.

Prompt:

Journaling gives your thoughts a place to land so they stop running you. What thoughts have been pacing your mind because they had nowhere safe to land? Let them rest here. Write without editing. Let the page hold what your mind no longer has to carry. What shifts when your thoughts are witnessed instead of contained inside you?

22. I'm Fine (Unsaid)

The performance gets heavy.

Prompt:
Where are you performing "I'm fine" while quietly unraveling? Be specific. No filters.

23. Silent Survival

When strength stopped making noise.

Prompt:
When did survival stop being loud and start becoming silent? What did that silence cost you?

24. Functioning Through the Fall

Not all breakdowns look broken.

Prompt:
What part of you learned to function through the fall? What did it hide to keep you standing?

24. When No One is Watching

Private truths hit different.

Prompt:
What does falling apart look like when no one is watching?

25. Fear Had Its Moment

It spoke. You answered.

Prompt:
Fear had its moment. You kept yours. What moment are you
reclaiming right now?

26. Momentum > Fear

Movement changes everything.

Prompt:
What has fear talked you out of that momentum is now pulling you back toward?

____
____
____
____
____
____
____
____
____
____
____
____
____
____
____
____
____
____
____
____
____
____
____
____
____
____

27. If You Moved Anyway

Imperfect still counts.

Prompt:
If you moved anyway — shaky, unfinished, unsure — what would actually change?

28. Who Defined "Crazy"

Labels stick when repeated.

Prompt:
Who taught you what "crazy" means — and why did you believe them?

29. Mislabeled, Not Understood

There's a difference.

Prompt:
Where has your mind been mislabeled instead of understood?

30. Drowned Truths

Silence has a sound.

Prompt:
What truth did you drown before you learned how to speak it?

31. Listening Instead of Numbing

There was another way all along.

Prompt:
What did you use to quiet yourself before you learned how to listen?

32. Soft Is Not Weak

Gentle doesn't mean unguarded.

Prompt:
Where in your life have you learned that softness was dangerous? What would it look like to be soft without shrinking, open without surrendering, and gentle without losing your edge?

33. I Didn't Break – I Bent

Pressure didn't destroy me, it reshaped me.

Prompt:

What moment did you think broke you, but actually taught you flexibility? How did bending keep you alive when standing rigid would have cost you everything?

34. This Is Where I Set Boundaries

Not all doors deserve my energy.

Prompt:

What boundary are you finally willing to enforce — even if it disappoints someone else? Who benefits when you don't protect your peace?

35. When Survival Got Quiet

Loud survival is easy to explain. Quiet survival isn't.

Prompt:
When did surviving stop looking dramatic and start becoming invisible? What quiet habits are currently keeping you alive?

36. The Version They Never Met

Not everyone earns access to your becoming.

Prompt:
Who only knows an outdated version of you? What parts of your
growth happened without witnesses — and why was that necessary?

37. I Trust My Timing Now

Delayed doesn't mean denied.

Prompt:
Where did impatience once cost you clarity? How has trusting your own timing protected you from moving too soon — or staying too long?

38. Still Here, Still Becoming

Progress doesn't require a finish line.

Prompt:
What does "being in progress" look like in this season of your life?
Where can you offer yourself grace instead of deadlines?

39. What I No Longer Explain

Explanation is not owed.

Prompt:
What truth about you are you done justifying? How does it feel to let
people misunderstand you — and move anyway?

40. I Made Peace With the Mirror

Reflection doesn't require perfection.

Prompt:

When you look at yourself now, what do you see that you didn't see before? What version of you finally feels familiar — even if unfinished?

41. No Reset. Only Forward

Nothing here was wasted.

Prompt:
What experiences once felt like detours but now make sense as preparation? How does it feel to realize you are continuing a story — not restarting one?

42. Stillness Isn't Safety

Pausing doesn't always mean peace.

Prompt:
Where in your life have you mistaken stillness for healing? What would gentle movement look like instead?

43. Safe Doesn't Mean Weak

Choosing safety is choosing self-respect.

Prompt:
What boundaries are you setting now that once felt like failure — but are actually strength?

44. Fear Had Its Moment

You didn't disappear. You recalibrated.

Prompt:
What moment are you reclaiming right now — and how are you stepping back into it differently?

45. Momentum Looks Good on Me

Progress doesn't have to be loud to be real.

Prompt:
Where are you moving forward quietly? How does that feel in your body?

46. Healing Has a Rhythm

Everything doesn't heal at once.

Prompt:
What pace does your healing need right now — and what happens when you honor it?

47. I'm Not Late, I'm On Time

Timing isn't failure. It's intelligence.

Prompt:
What arrived later than expected but right when you were ready?

48. The Soft Comeback

Not all returns are dramatic.

Prompt:
How are you re-entering your life with more gentleness than before?

49. City Lights, Quiet Wins

Some victories don't need witnesses.

Prompt:
What have you survived or achieved that no one applauded — but
mattered deeply?

50. Nervous System, Meet Luxury

Peace can feel plush.

Prompt:
What calms you instantly? How can you offer yourself more of that?

51. Healing Without Announcements

You don't owe progress updates.

Prompt:
What are you working through privately — and why does that privacy matter?

52. Triggers Read Like Street Names

Awareness changes the route.

Prompt:
What patterns do you now recognize early — and how do you navigate them differently?

53. The Art of Not Explaining

Silence can be sovereign.

Prompt:
Where are you choosing not to defend, justify, or over-explain anymore?

54. Survival Gave Me Style

Grace under pressure is still grace.

Prompt:
How has surviving shaped your presence, confidence, or taste?

55. When Quiet Became Power

Peace doesn't need permission.

Prompt:
When did you realize that being quieter made you stronger?

56. My Mind Is Not the Enemy

It carried you this far.

Prompt:
Where have you judged your mind instead of listening to it?

57. Rewriting "Crazy"

Labels are lazy.

Prompt:

How has your depth, sensitivity, or intuition been misunderstood —
and what's the truer story?

58. A Place for My Thoughts to Land

Containment is kindness.

Prompt:
What does journaling give you that holding everything inside never could?

59. Progress Without Pressure

You don't need urgency to move.

Prompt:
Where can you release the need to "hurry" your healing?

60. I Trust Myself Again

That's the real breakthrough.

Prompt:
What helped you begin trusting your instincts after doubting them?

61. I Don't Chase Peace. I Practice It

Consistency over chaos.

Prompt:
What daily habits help you stay grounded, even on hard days?

62. I'm Allowed to Rest Mid-Journey

Exhaustion isn't a badge of honor.

Prompt:
Where do you need rest — not as retreat, but as strategy?

____
____
____
____
____
____
____
____
____
____
____
____
____
____
____
____
____
____
____
____
____
____
____
____
____
____
____
____
____
____

63. No Arrival, Just Becoming

You're already in motion.

Prompt:
What parts of yourself are still unfolding — and how can you enjoy the process?

64. Movement > Stillness

I learned when to wait — and when to move. Stillness didn't save me.
Movement did.

Prompt:

Nothing grows without movement. What forward-moving steps will speak more peace as a love language to yourself?

65. I Didn't Disappear. I Adjusted.

Growth doesn't always look loud. Sometimes it looks like restraint.

Prompt:
Where in your life did growth ask you to shift instead of shine? How have your recent adjustments protected your peace, preserved your energy, or redirected your path? Write about the ways you've evolved quietly — and why that matters.

66. Fear Showed Up. I Stayed.

I didn't rush. I didn't freeze. I chose myself. Timing doesn't ask permission. It asks for courage. What I carry forward now is mine to protect.

Prompt

What moment in your life did fear try to steal —your voice, your confidence, your next step? Where did you hesitate, pause, or go quiet because it felt safer than moving? Now tell the truth: What part of you stayed anyway? What did you protect, preserve, or refuse to surrender — even while scared? Write about the moment you didn't disappear. You might not have been loud – but you were present. That counts.

67. Masterpiece, Still Drying

Art doesn't rush itself.

Prompt:
What makes you proud of who you're becoming —even unfinished?

68. Momentum Over Fear

Even gentle movement counts.

Prompt:

Today, I choose forward — even if it's quiet, even if it's imperfect. This moment matters too. I am present now. In what ways can you recognize forward movement in your life's decisions, even when it doesn't look dramatic?

69. My Pace. My Timing. My Power.

Timing is not weakness. It's wisdom.

Prompt:

I honor my rhythm. I trust my process. What's meant for me cannot miss me. In what ways are you practicing patience with your life's movement while staying present in the moment.

70. Masterpiece in Progress

Unfinished does not mean unworthy.

Prompt:

I am becoming — and that is enough. I don't wait to feel "finished" to live fully. How can you live more mindfully in the present to nourish your purest, most authentic self?

Epilogue

Healing isn't a finish line. It's a practice.

For some of us, the work of rebuilding happens quietly—decision by decision, boundary by boundary, breath by breath.

There were seasons when silence and stigma tried to define my story. They didn't get the last word.

These pages were never about writing perfectly. They were about creating space for reflection, healing, and personal truth.

If these prompts helped you pause, listen inward, or understand yourself more deeply, then they have served their purpose.

Keep writing.
Keep reflecting.
Keep becoming.

Acknowledgments

This season of my life is quieter and more intentional. I am more private now—more protective, more grounded. Still, growth is never as solitary as it sometimes feels.

To the loved ones who stood with me, sometimes close and sometimes at a distance, thank you. Your presence mattered more than you know.

To the professionals who offered language and structure when life felt unstable, thank you. Your guidance helped shape this path.

To the spiritual voices who reminded me that faith and psychology do not compete, thank you. Recovery did not shrink my life—it strengthened it.

And to every reader who opens these pages and chooses reflection, healing, and personal truth—thank you for walking part of this road with me.

— JAI Lewis

Meet the Author

About the Author

JAI Lewis is a memoirist whose work explores the intersection of mental health, addiction, recovery, faith, and identity. Her writing is grounded in decades of navigating bipolar disorder, cultural silence, self-advocacy, and the daily discipline of stability.

Raised in an educated family unprepared for the complexities of a psychiatric diagnosis, she learned in real time what recovery requires—not just understanding, but participation.

Through therapy, treatment, and what she calls "soul work," she rebuilt her relationship with her mind, her body, and her life.

Whiskey Prayers and Midnight Moments is her debut memoir. *Whiskey Prayers: The Journal* continues that work by inviting readers into reflection, healing, and personal truth through guided writing.

She is currently working on her next book, *Scarred Gold*.

Book Club Invitation

Thank you for reading *Whiskey Prayers and Midnight Moments*.

If your book club selects this memoir, I would love to hear about your conversation and reflections. This story was written not just to be read, but to spark honest dialogue about healing, mental health, resilience, and the power of rebuilding a life.

Readers and book clubs are welcome to share their discussions and thoughts online using the hashtag #WhiskeyPrayers.

Your voices, stories, and perspectives help keep the conversation going.

9 798995 331728